When a Pet Dies

FIRST EXPERIENCES

When a Pet Dies

BY FRED ROGERS

photographs by Jim Judkis

Penguin Young Readers Group

With special thanks to: Nan Earl Newell;
Margaret B. McFarland, Ph.D., Senior Consultant;
Barry N. Head; the Janes family; the Savido family;
Dr. Larry Gerson; the Western Pennsylvania Humane Society;
and the other parents and children who agreed
to help us with the book.

Library of Congress Cataloging-in-Publication Data
Rogers, Fred. When a pet dies. (A Mister Rogers' First experience book)
Summary: Explores the feelings of frustration, sadness, and loneliness that
a youngster may feel when a pet dies.
1. Children and death—Juvenile literature. 2. Bereavement—Juvenile literature.
3. Pets—Death—Psychological aspects—Juvenile literature. [1. Pets—Death. 2.
Death] I. Judkis, Jim, ill. II. Title. III. Series: Rogers, Fred. Mister Rogers' First
experience book. BF723.D3R64   1988   155.9'37   87-18207
ISBN 978-0-698-11666-5
20   19   18   17   16   15   14

When I was little and didn't have a sister yet, my best friend was a brown, wire-haired mongrel named Mitzi. We shared joyous times, exciting times and sad times. We got scared together when there was thunder and lightning, and together we crawled under the bed until they went away. When I wasn't scared of them any more, Mitzi still was, so I comforted her and felt all the braver.

When Mitzi died I was very sad, and so were my parents. We had lost a member of the family. My parents encouraged me to talk about how I felt, and they let me know that grieving was a natural, healing thing to do. In grieving, we try to fill the empty space that was created in us by the loss. Because of Mitzi I discovered it was all right to cry when somebody you love dies. I learned, too, that loss takes time to understand.

Like other First Experience books, this one is created to encourage family talk. As you and your children look at the photos and read the text, I hope you'll find it possible to share your real feelings about a pet's dying. As for what happens *after* death, I believe that's best discussed in light of each family's traditions and beliefs. Those traditions and beliefs are important things to share with your children if and when they ask!

Since all living things die at one time or another, I trust that this First Experience book will be of service to you beyond the death of a pet.

—Fred Rogers

A pet can be a very important part of your life.

That pet can be like a
friend you play with
and help take care of.

Caring for a pet isn't always
easy. It's different from caring
for a teddy bear or a toy.

Toys and teddy bears don't get sick . . . except
for pretend . . . so they don't need doctors.

But real animals
sometimes do get sick.

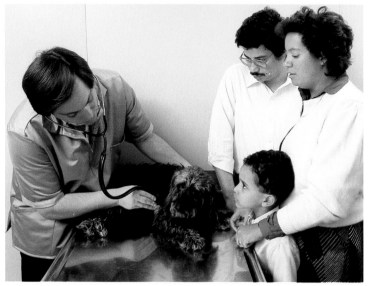

Sick pets may need special doctors called "veterinarians" or "vets." Vets know a lot about animals and the best ways to help them stay well.

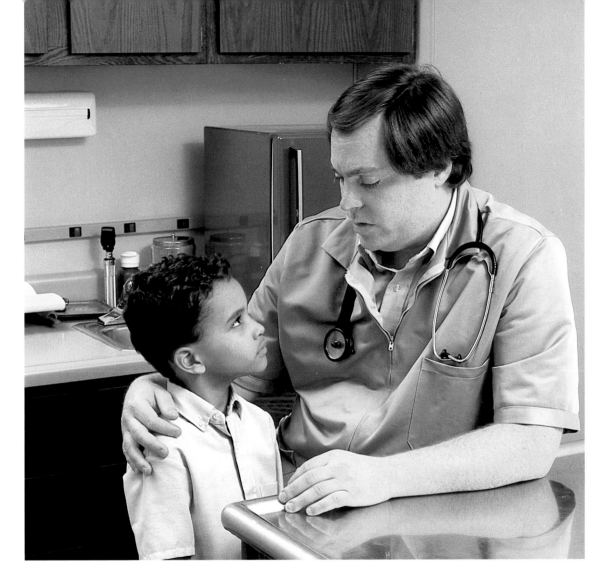

But even when a pet has had the very best care, there comes a time when it might be too sick or too badly hurt or maybe just too old for you, or anyone, *even* the vet, to be able to keep it alive.

It can be very hard when a pet you love dies. You may feel that you'll never stop being sad, that the hurt will never go away . . . but it will.

Missing your pet can make you feel lonely.

You *may* feel so sad that you even cry a lot.

You *might* feel angry and wonder why such a sad thing had to happen.

It isn't always easy to talk about sad and angry feelings, but talking to someone you love can help the hurt go away.

You might have questions to ask that person, too . . . like "What *is* dying?" That's something everyone wonders about.

One thing we know about dying is that it isn't like
going to sleep. When something alive goes to sleep,
it can wake up again. When a pet dies, it isn't alive
anymore, so it can't wake up again. A pet that dies
stops breathing and moving. It doesn't see or hear
anymore. And it doesn't need to eat anymore.

People often wish they could have done something to stop their pets from dying . . . even when there was nothing they could have done. Or they might wish they could find a way to make their pet come alive again—even though that can't happen.

When pets die, their bodies are often put in a box
and buried in the ground. Sometimes the vet takes
care of the burying and sometimes it's the people
who lived with the pet who do it. Often they bury
their pet in a special place.

They may even want to mark the place where their pet is buried.

Lots of people find it helps to get together and
have a ceremony when they bury a dead pet. That's
called a "funeral." Funerals are times when people
can feel sad together and feel better together and
remember the happier times together.

People don't always like to be with someone else when they feel sad. A person might like to be alone for a while.

No matter how sad or angry you feel when your pet dies, one thing you can be sure of is that you won't always feel that way.

When sad things do happen, the best place
to be is near someone you love . . . someone
who can understand how you are feeling.

There will come a time when your sadness and anger
have gone away . . . a time when you can feel happy again
about the good times you and your pet had together.

After a while, you may even feel that you
want to have *another* pet.

You and the people you love can talk about those feelings. You'll all know when you're ready.

Happy times and sad times are part of everyone's life.
When a pet dies, we can grow to know that the love
we shared is still alive in us and always will be.